leased when the living spaces need it. To do so, you distribute the heat via natural convection by opening the sliding glass doors that connect the greenhouse with the den *(see plans)* and with the living room. Unwanted sun can be blocked out at any time by a roll-down shade. But if excess heat should accumulate, you can get rid of it by opening the vent along the top edge of the greenhouse.

Backup heating (and cooling) is supplied by an electric heat pump.

Lots of open spaces and partial ceilings maximize airflow. Study the photos of the areas just inside the greenhouse—the living room *(bottom right photo)* and the den *(pictured upper left)*—and you can trace the path of the heated greenhouse air as it flows past the open sliders and rises

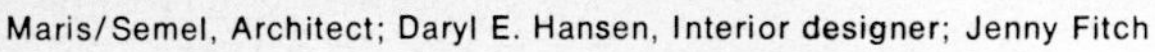

Maris/Semel, Architect; Daryl E. Hansen, Interior designer; Jenny Fitch

CUSTOM REVERSED PLANS NOT AVAILABLE FOR THIS DESIGN.

through the joist spaces in the ceiling. Air from the second level drops down the opposite side of the house and completes the loop to the lower reaches of the greenhouse, ready to soak up some more heat and make another cycle.

A sweeping panorama of the living/dining/kitchen area greets you when you step through the entry.

Right around the corner from the kitchen is the master bedroom *(bottom left photo).* On the second level two children's bedrooms are separated by a central bath. For optimum airflow, the sidewalls should be open railings; however, if you want more privacy, you can fill in the walls and install a series of large vents.

design

49-1170

ENERGY EFFICIENT HOME

3 BEDROOM PLAN

Living Area Plan 1 & 2
First Floor . . . . 1,147 Sq. Ft.
Second Floor. . . . . . . 530 Sq. Ft.

PLEASE SPECIFY PLAN 1 OR PLAN 2 WHEN ORDERING BLUEPRINT PLANS.

- Compact floor plan makes maximum use of space.
- Vaulted ceiling living room and master bedroom.
- Centrally located U-shaped kitchen with pass-through to breakfast space.
- Deluxe baths on both floors.
- Spacious garage with room for workshop or storage.

SECOND FLOOR

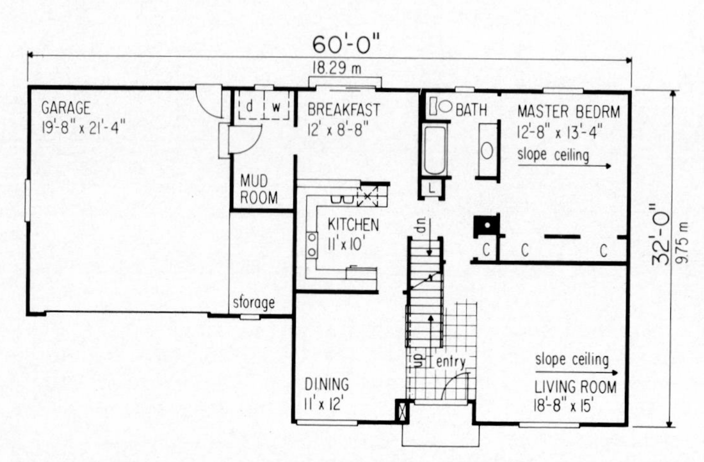

FIRST FLOOR PLAN 1 WITH BASEMENT

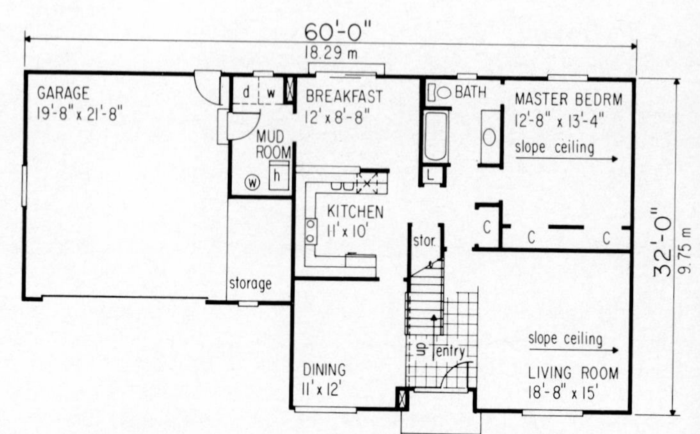

FIRST FLOOR PLAN 2 WITHOUT BASEMENT

FRONT VIEW

REAR VIEW

Living Area
Plan 1 & 2 . . . . 1,500 Sq. Ft.

2-3 BEDROOM PLAN

design 49-1174

ENERGY EFFICIENT HOME

- Designed for energy efficiency, the open floor plan provides for fast and efficient air and heat circulation.
- When oriented to the north, the garage and earth berming serve as a buffer against the cold north wind.
- Minimum north facing glass and air-lock type entry help reduce home heating requirements.
- South facing living room and bedrooms obtain maximum amount of light and warmth from the winter sun.

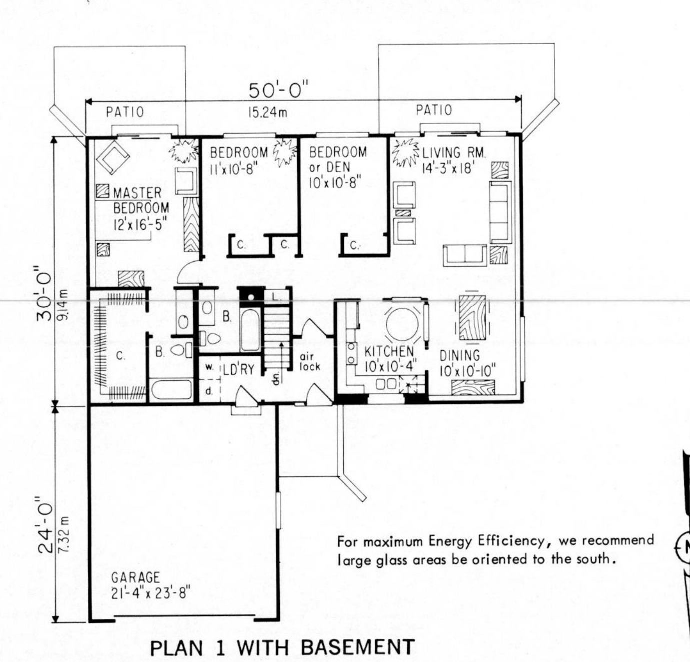

PLAN 1 WITH BASEMENT

For maximum Energy Efficiency, we recommend large glass areas be oriented to the south.

N

50'-0" 15.24m PATIO PATIO MASTER BEDROOM 12'x16'-5" BEDROOM 11'x10'-8" BEDROOM or DEN 10'x10'-8" LIVING RM 14'-3"x18' KITCHEN 10'x10'-4" DINING 10'x10'-10" UTILITY air lock GARAGE 21'-4"x 23'-8" 30'-0" 9.14m 24'-0" 7.32 m

PLAN 2 WITHOUT BASEMENT

design

49-1175

ENERGY EFFICIENT HOME

3 BEDROOM PLAN

Living Area
Plan 1 & 2 . . . . 1,424 Sq. Ft.

- Vaulted ceiling Great Room with off-center exposed ridge beam.
- Vaulted ceiling foyer and sheltered entrance.
- Two car garage with space for workshop or storage.
- Spacious kitchen, adjacent to laundry room.

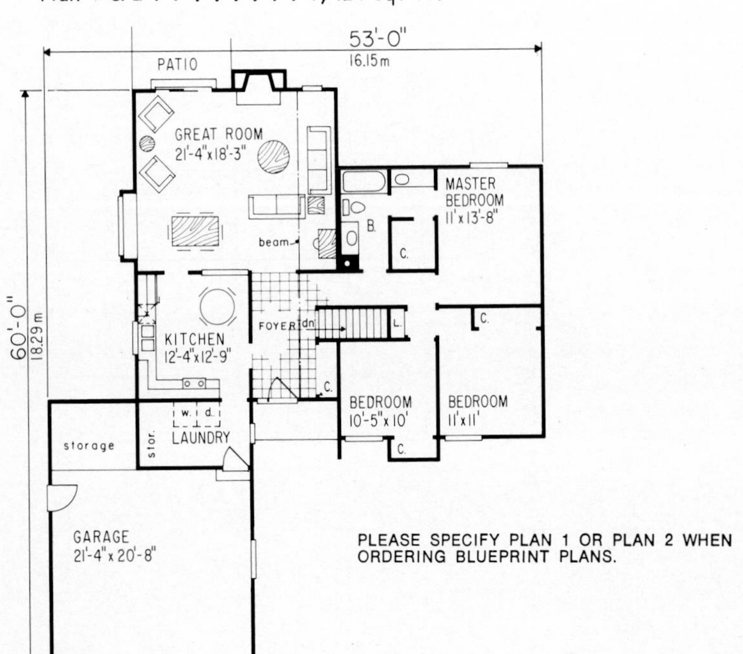

PLAN 1 WITH BASEMENT

PLEASE SPECIFY PLAN 1 OR PLAN 2 WHEN ORDERING BLUEPRINT PLANS.

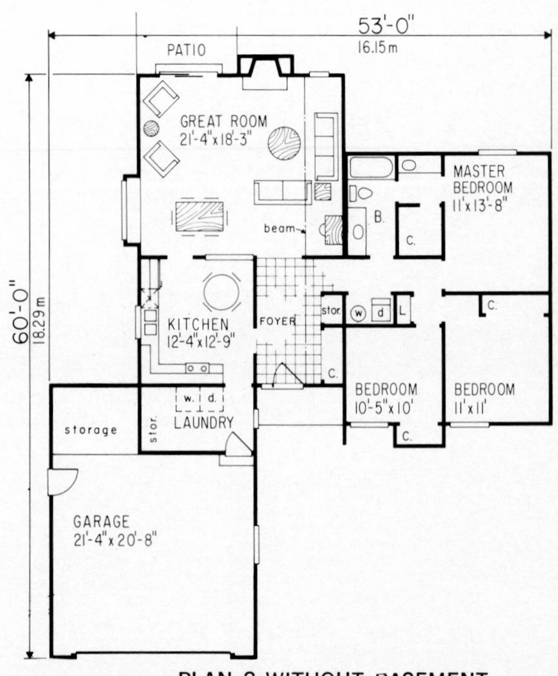

PLAN 2 WITHOUT BASEMENT

Living Area
Plan 1 & 2 . . . 1,400 Sq. Ft.

Artists' renderings & floor plans may vary slightly from actual working drawings.

PLEASE SPECIFY PLAN 1 OR PLAN 2 WHEN ORDERING BLUEPRINT PLANS.

For maximum Energy Efficiency, we recommend large glass areas to be oriented to the south.

design 49-1176

ENERGY EFFICIENT HOME

3 BEDROOM PLAN

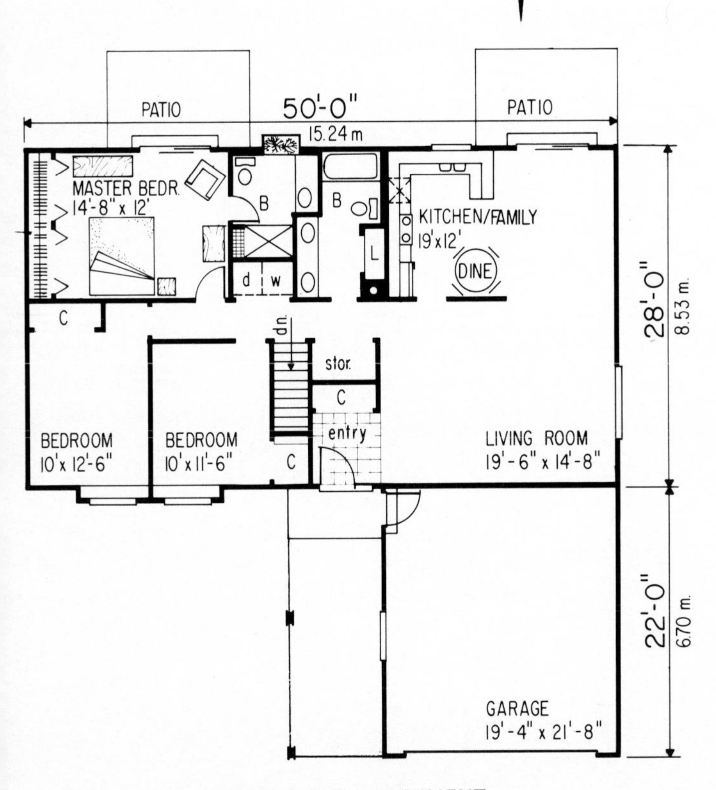

PLAN 1 WITH BASEMENT

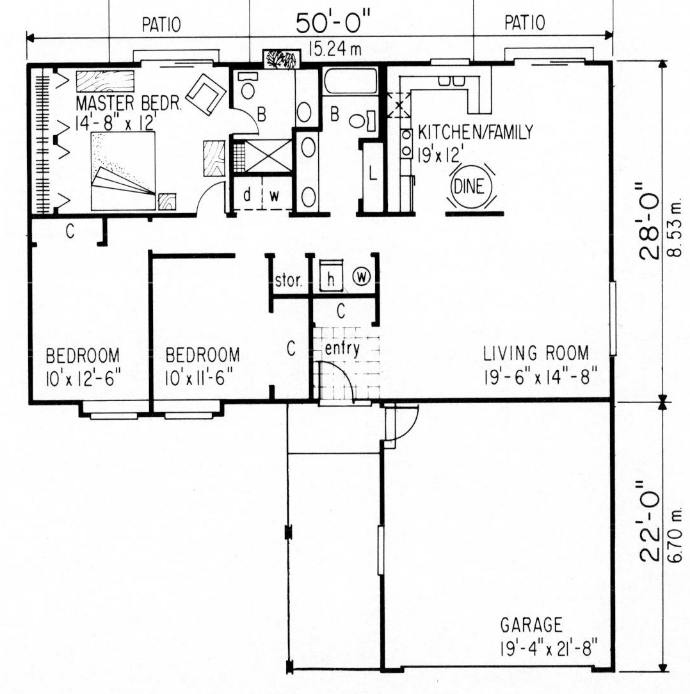

PLAN 2 WITHOUT BASEMENT

design
49-1177

ENERGY EFFICIENT HOME

Living Area Plan 1 & 2 . . . 1,021 Sq. Ft.
Future Bedroom Addition . . . 288 Sq. Ft.

Artists' renderings & floor plans may vary slightly from actual working drawings.

2-3 BEDROOM PLAN

PLEASE SPECIFY PLAN 1 OR PLAN 2 WHEN ORDERING BLUEPRINT PLANS.

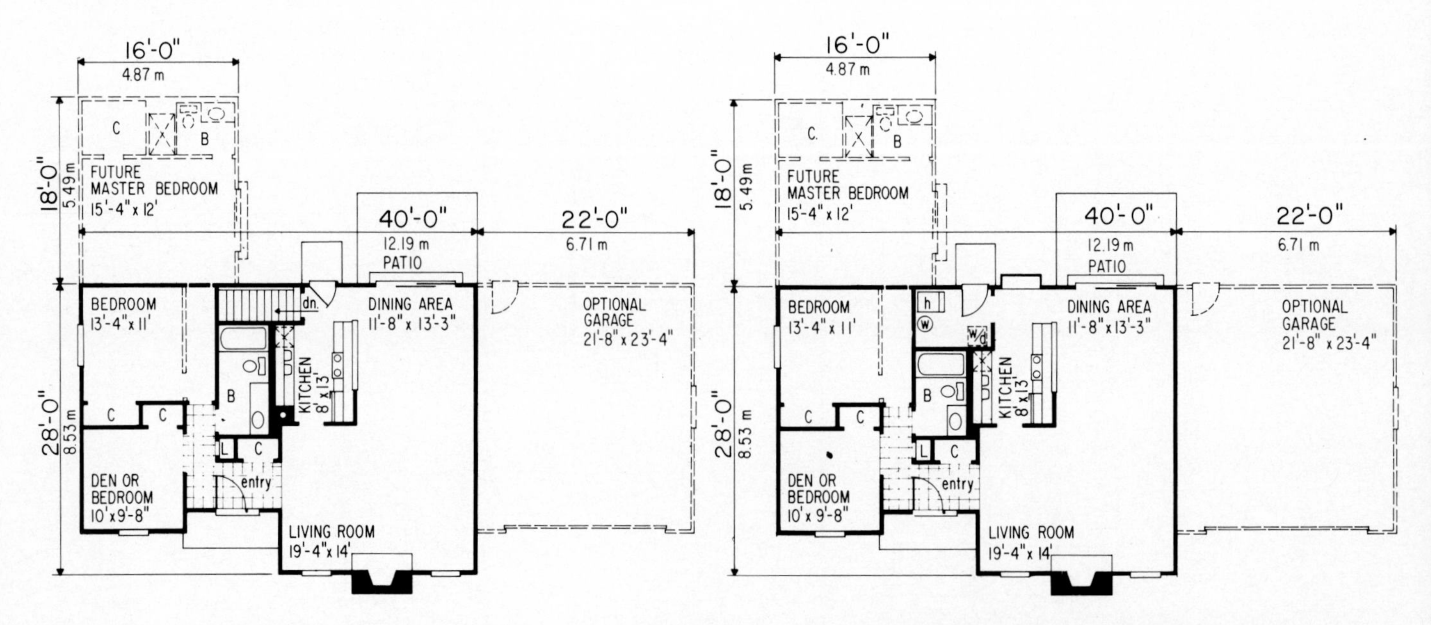

PLAN 1 WITH BASEMENT

PLAN 2 WITHOUT BASEMENT

design
49-1182

ENERGY EFFICIENT HOME

2-3 BEDROOM PLAN

Living Area Plan 1 or 2 . .
First Floor . . . . 1,088 Sq. Ft.
Second Floor . . . . . . 612 Sq. Ft.

PLEASE SPECIFY PLAN 1 OR PLAN 2 WHEN ORDERING BLUEPRINT PLANS.

- Contemporary styling
- Designed for informal living with vaulted ceiling Great Room.
- First floor den or bedroom option.
- When oriented to the south, the large expanse of glass and skylights in the Great Room plus second floor clerestory windows allow for the collection of warmth from the winter's sun.

For maximum Energy Efficiency, we recommend large glass areas to be oriented to the south.

N

MASTER BEDROOM 15'x12'-3"
open to great room
railing
clerestory above
dn
B.
BEDROOM 15'x10'-8"

SECOND FLOOR

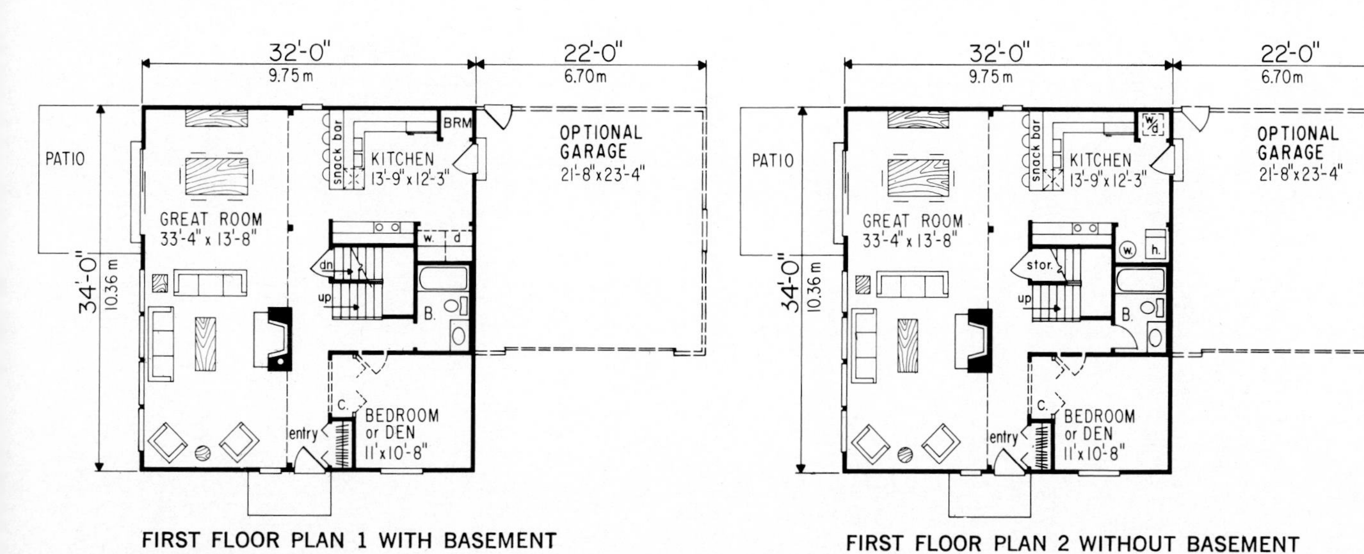

FIRST FLOOR PLAN 1 WITH BASEMENT

FIRST FLOOR PLAN 2 WITHOUT BASEMENT

design
49-1183

ENERGY EFFICIENT HOME

Living Area

First Floor (Plan 1)	1,187 Sq. Ft.
Second Floor	730 Sq. Ft.
First Floor (Plan 2)	1,210 Sq. Ft.
Second Floor	730 Sq. Ft.

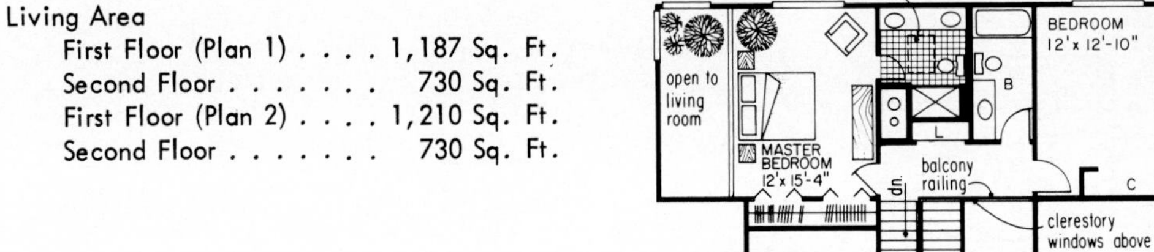

3 BEDROOM PLAN

- Open plan with living room open to second floor.
- Vaulted Foyer, stairwell and second floor hall receive daylight from skylight and clerestory windows.
- Minimum windows on north elevation plus garage buffer help keep heating cost down.
- Greenhouse type solarium and large glass areas on south elevation help absorb both light and warmth from the sun in winter months.

For maximum Energy Efficiency, we recommend large glass areas to be oriented to the south.

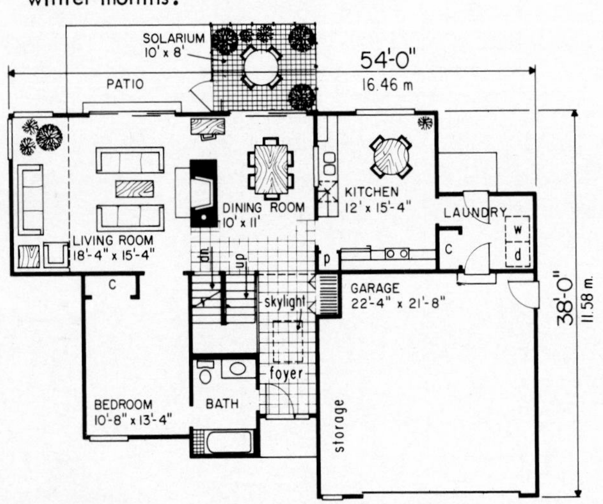

FIRST FLOOR PLAN 1 WITH BASEMENT

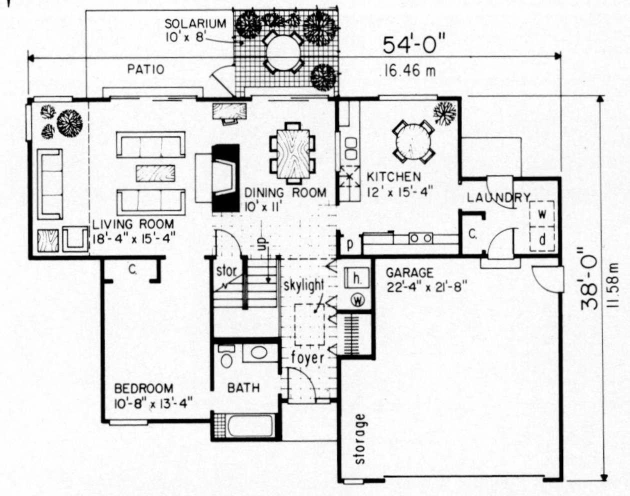

FIRST FLOOR PLAN 2 WITHOUT BASEMENT

Living Area
Main & Upper .... 1,004 Sq. Ft.
Lower Level .... 528 Sq. Ft.

Artists' renderings & floor plans may vary slightly from actual working drawings.

design
49-ES-152

ENERGY EFFICIENT HOME

3 BEDROOM PLAN

BLUEPRINT PLANS AVAILABLE

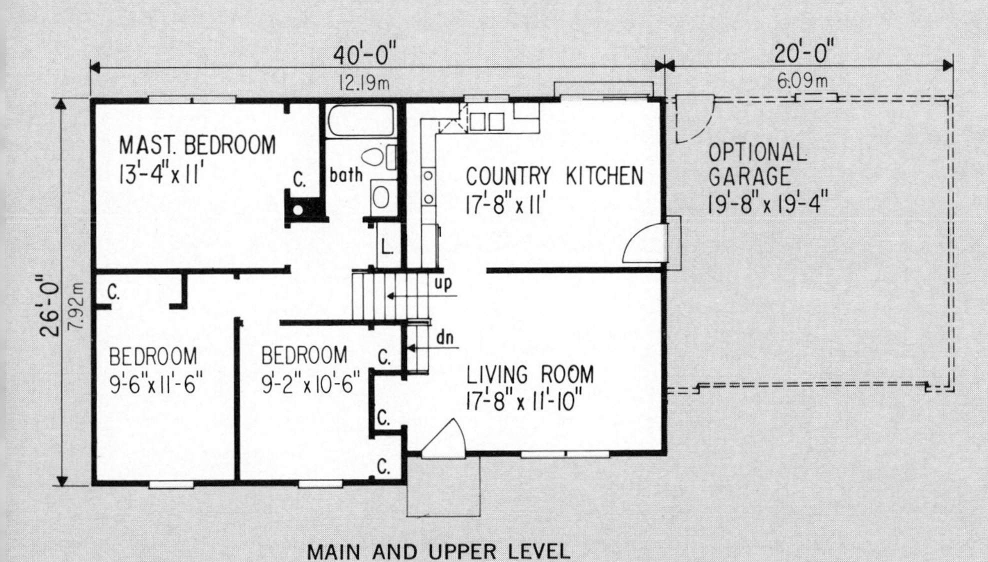

MAIN AND UPPER LEVEL

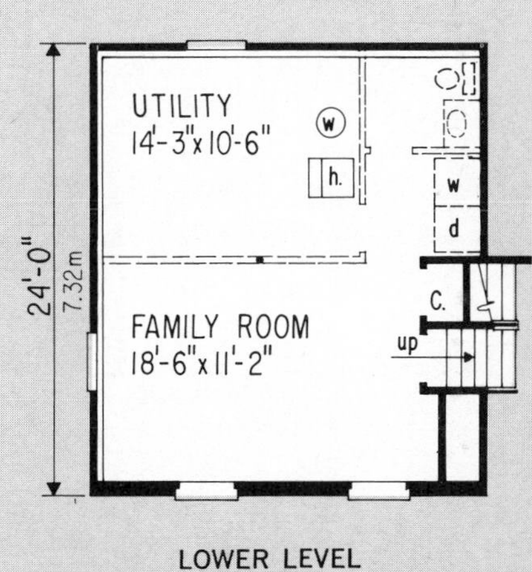

LOWER LEVEL

design
ARLINGTON
ENERGY EFFICIENT HOME
49-1171

Living Area
Plan 1 or 2 ...... 884 Sq. Ft.

Artists' renderings & floor plans may vary slightly from actual working drawings.

PLEASE SPECIFY PLAN 1 OR PLAN 2 WHEN ORDERING BLUEPRINT PLANS.

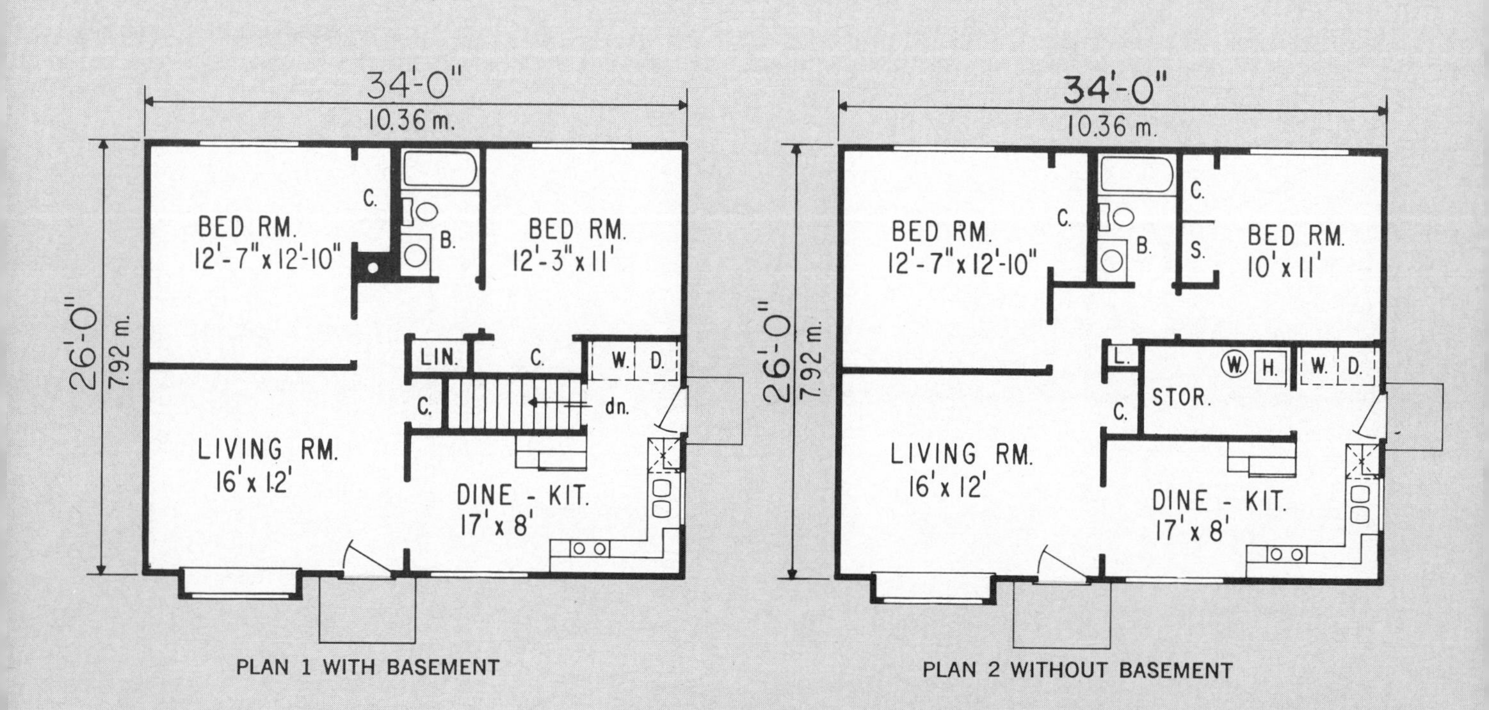

PLAN 1 WITH BASEMENT

PLAN 2 WITHOUT BASEMENT

design COLUMBUS

ENERGY EFFICIENT HOME
49-1172

3 BEDROOM PLAN

Living Area
Plan 1 or 2 .... 912 Sq. Ft.

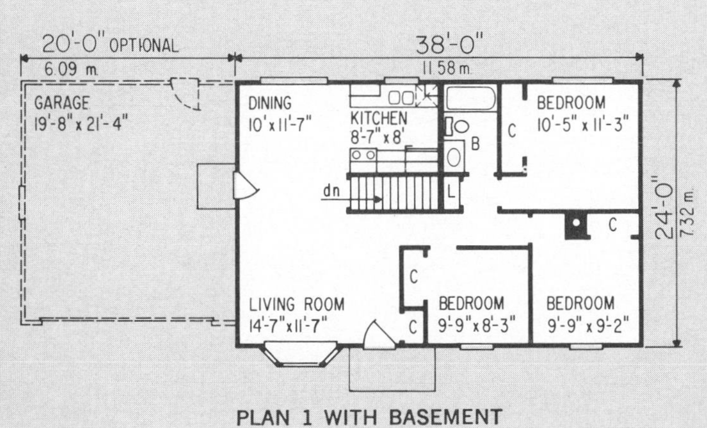

PLAN 1 WITH BASEMENT

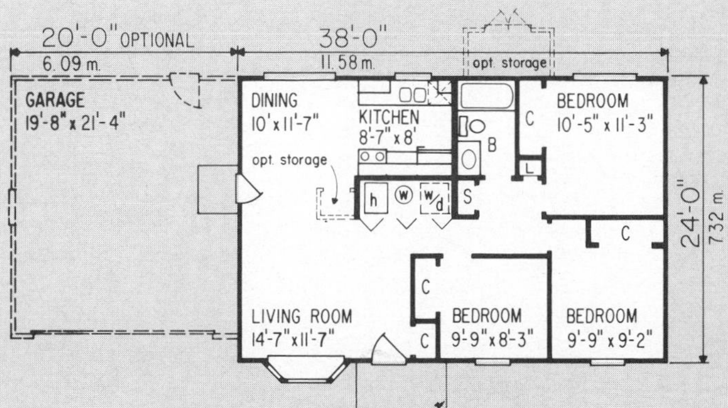

PLAN 2 WITHOUT BASEMENT

Artists' renderings & floor plans may vary slightly from actual working drawings.

PLEASE SPECIFY PLAN 1 OR PLAN 2 WHEN ORDERING BLUEPRINT PLANS.

design
FRANKFORT

ENERGY EFFICIENT HOME
49-1173

2-3-4 BEDROOM PLAN

Living Area
Main Level .... 923 Sq. Ft.
Lower Level ...... 876 Sq. Ft.

BLUEPRINT PLANS AVAILABLE

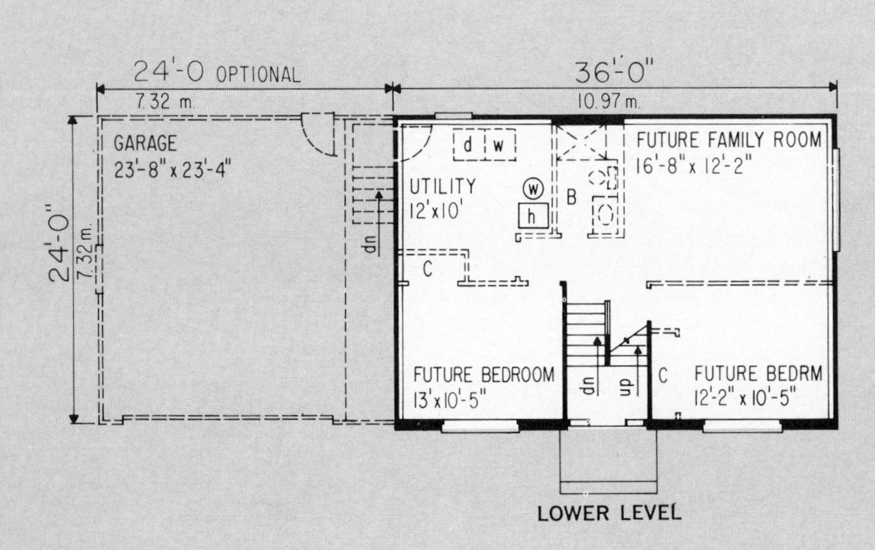

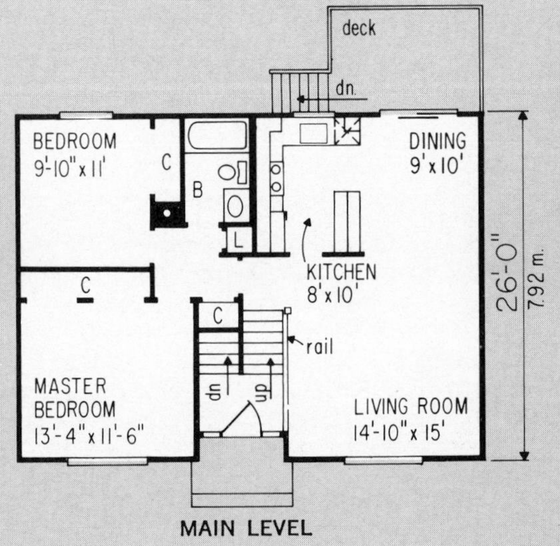

Artists' renderings & floor plans may vary slightly from actual working drawings.

design BARRINGTON

ENERGY EFFICIENT HOME
49-1178

3 BEDROOM PLAN

Living Area
Plan 1 or 2 .... 960 Sq. Ft.

PLEASE SPECIFY WITH OR WITHOUT BASEMENT
WHEN ORDERING BLUEPRINT PLANS

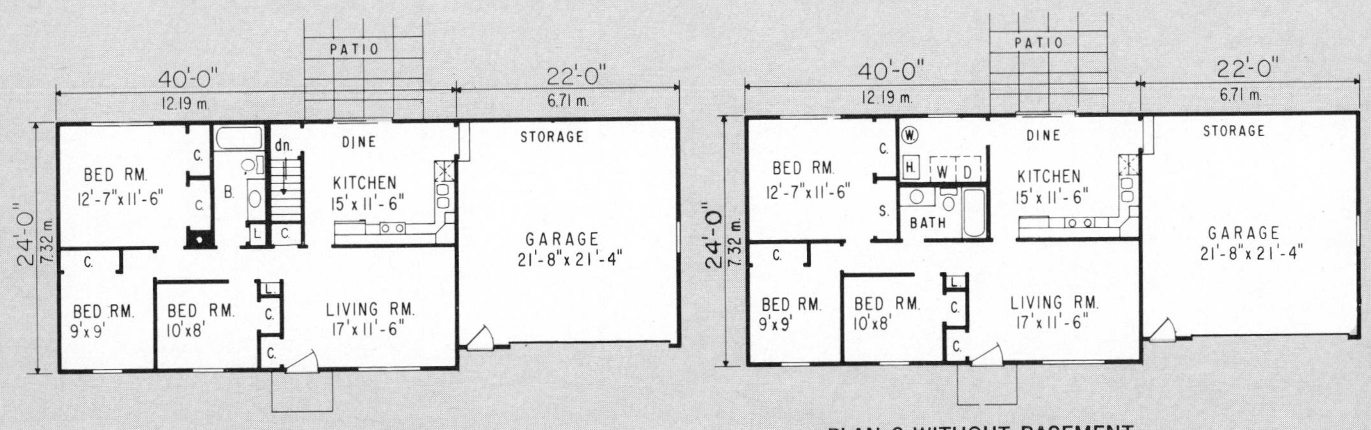

PLAN 1 WITH BASEMENT

PLAN 2 WITHOUT BASEMENT

design

SACRAMENTO

ENERGY EFFICIENT HOME
49-1179

Living Area .... 960 Sq. Ft.

3 BEDROOM PLAN

PLEASE SPECIFY PLAN 1 OR PLAN 2 WHEN ORDERING BLUEPRINT PLANS.

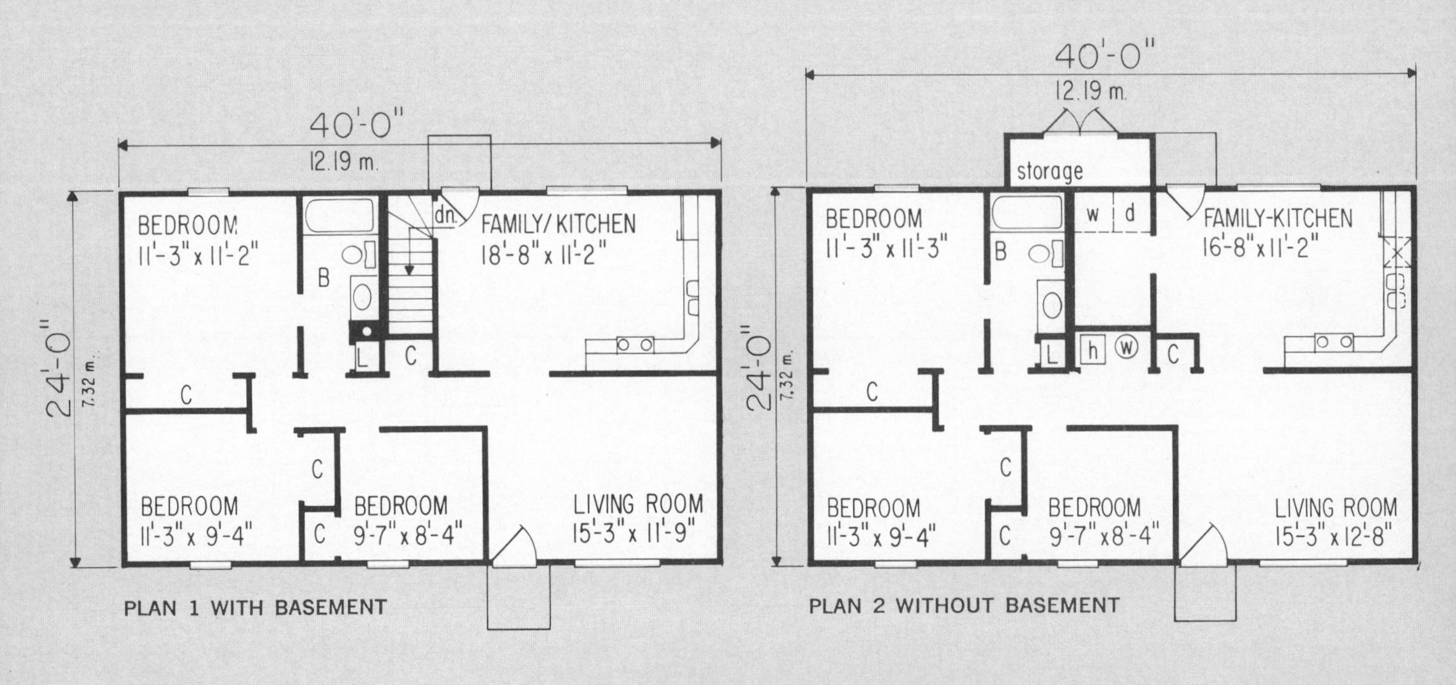

Living Area
Plan 1 or 2 .... 960 Sq. Ft.

design SPRINGFIELD

ENERGY EFFICIENT HOME
49-1180

3 BEDROOM PLAN

BLUEPRINT PLANS AVAILABLE

Artists' renderings & floor plans may vary slightly from actual working drawings.

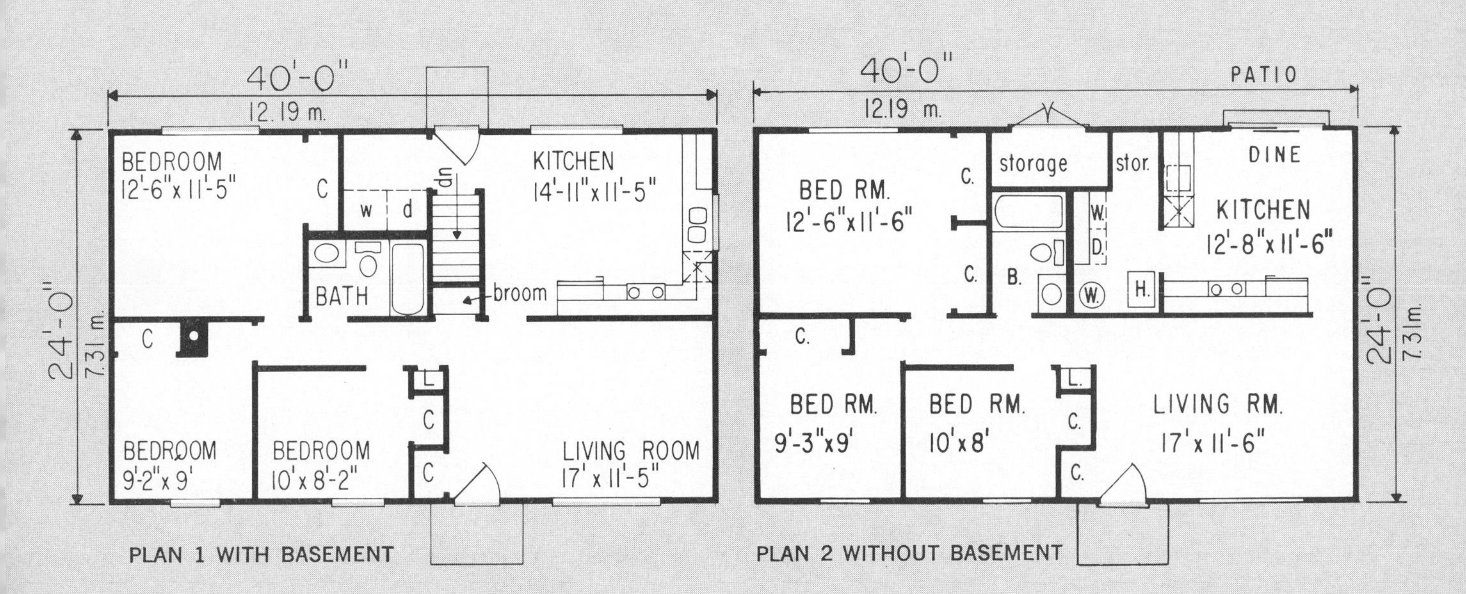

design
BIRMINGHAM

ENERGY EFFICIENT HOME
49-1181

3 BEDROOM PLAN

Living Area
Plan 1 or 2 .... 1,040 Sq. Ft.

PLEASE SPECIFY PLAN 1 OR PLAN 2 WHEN ORDERING BLUEPRINT PLANS.

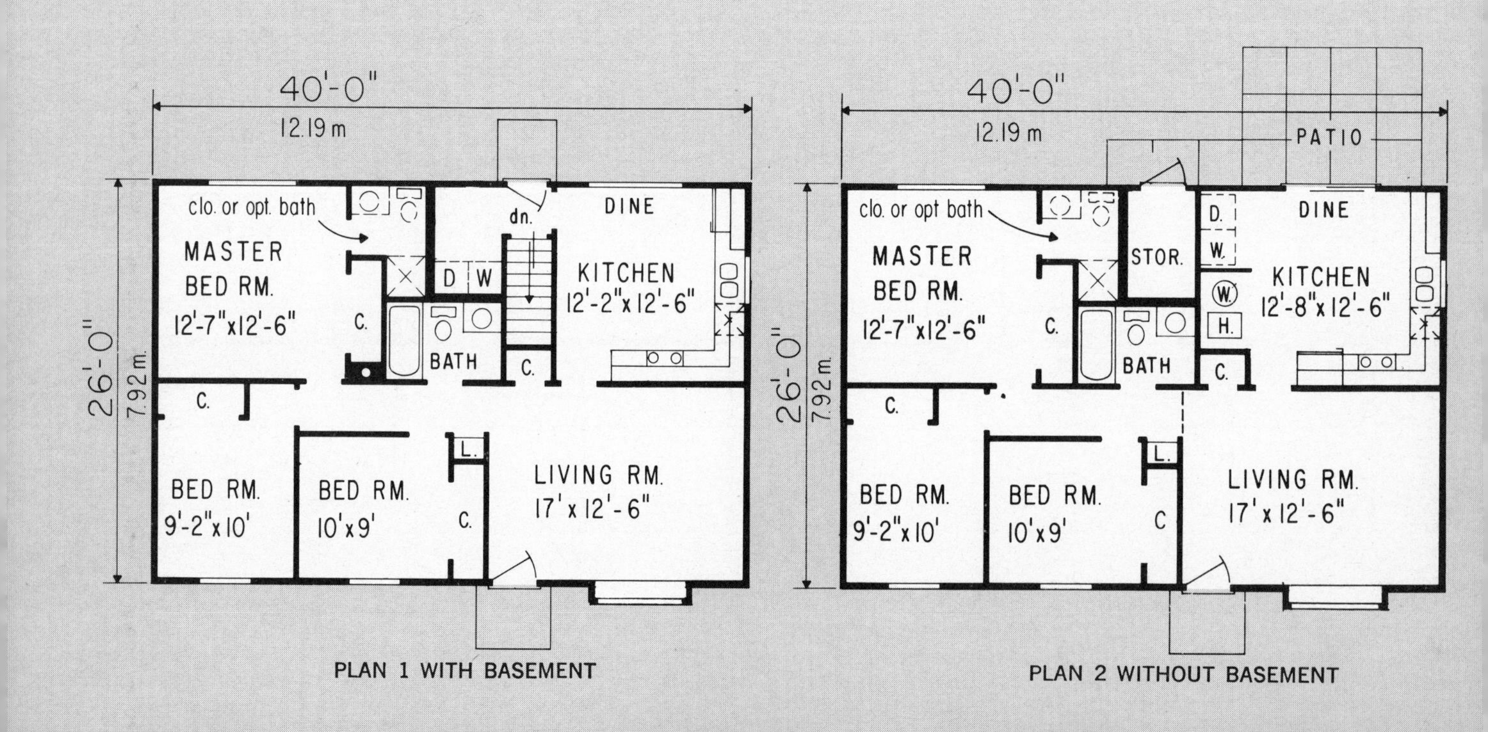

Living Area
Main Level ...... 1,040 Sq. Ft.
Lower Level ..... 1,040 Sq. Ft.

BLUEPRINT PLANS AVAILABLE

design
SCRANTON
ENERGY EFFICIENT HOME
49-1186

2-3-4 BEDROOM PLAN

Artists' renderings & floor plans may vary slightly from actual working drawings.

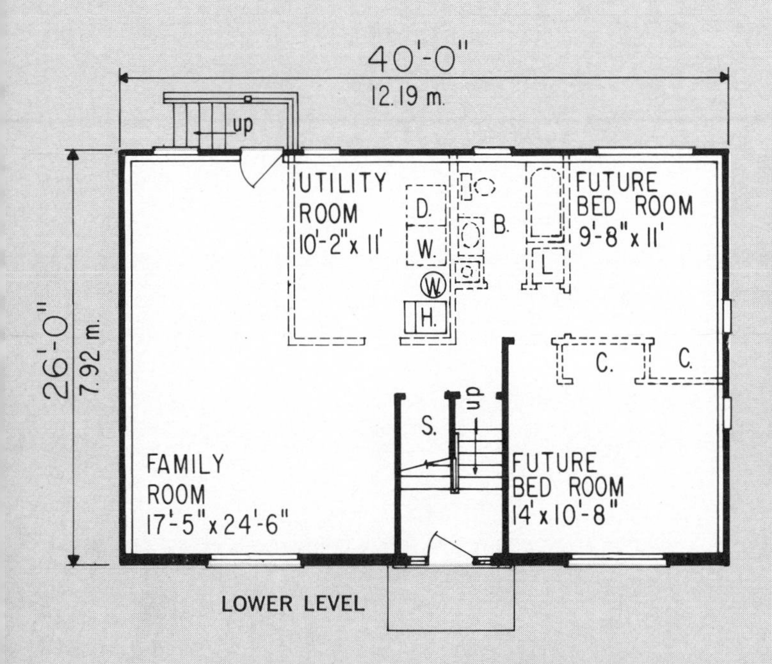

LOWER LEVEL

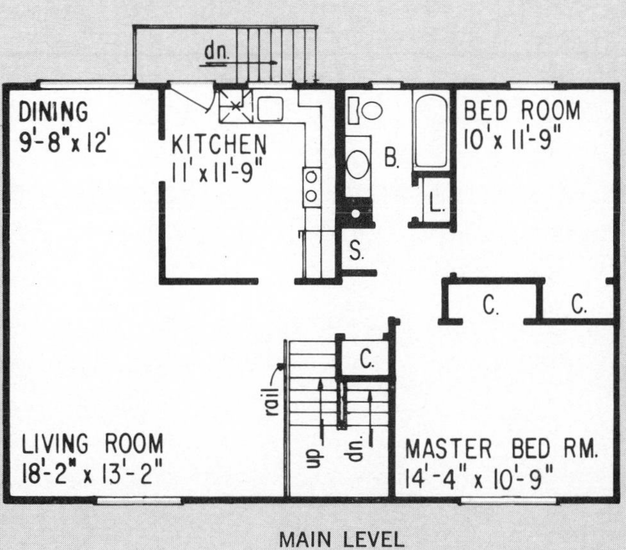

MAIN LEVEL

design

DAVENPORT

ENERGY EFFICIENT HOME
49-1187

.3 BEDROOM PLAN

Living Area
Plan 1 or 2 ...... 1,064 Sq. Ft.

PLEASE SPECIFY PLAN 1 OR PLAN 2 WHEN ORDERING BLUEPRINT PLANS.

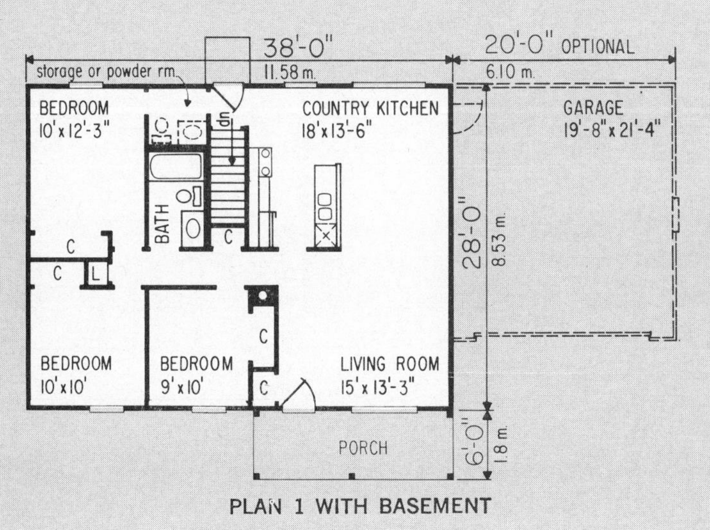

PLAN 1 WITH BASEMENT

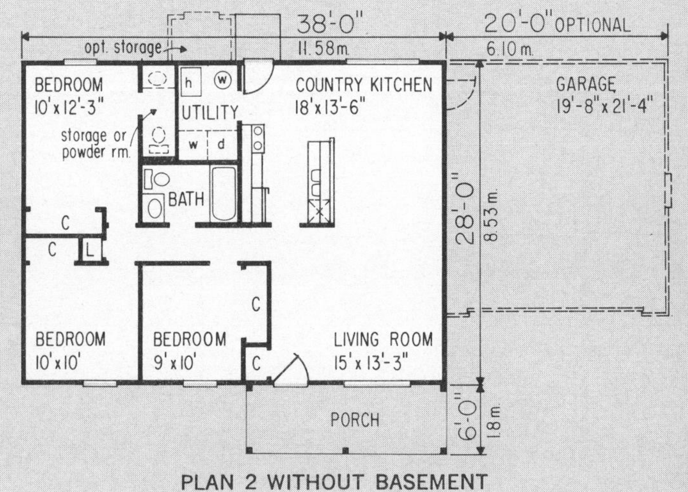

PLAN 2 WITHOUT BASEMENT

design HOUSTON

ENERGY EFFICIENT HOME
49-1188

3 BEDROOM PLAN

Living Area
Plan 1 or 2 ...... 1,096 Sq. Ft.

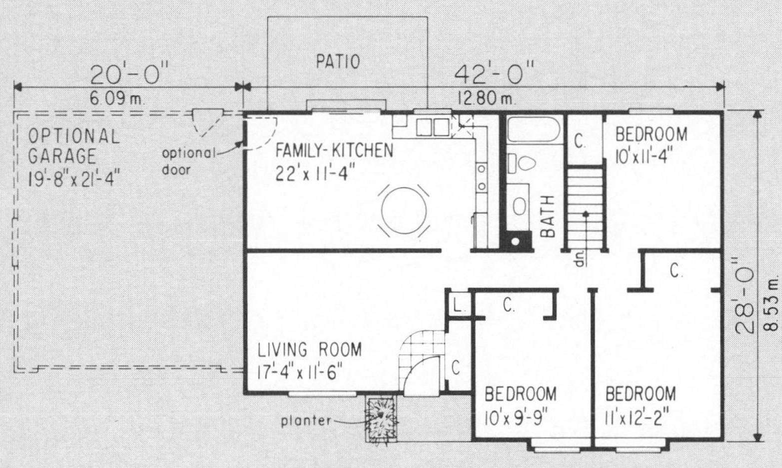

PLAN 1 WITH BASEMENT

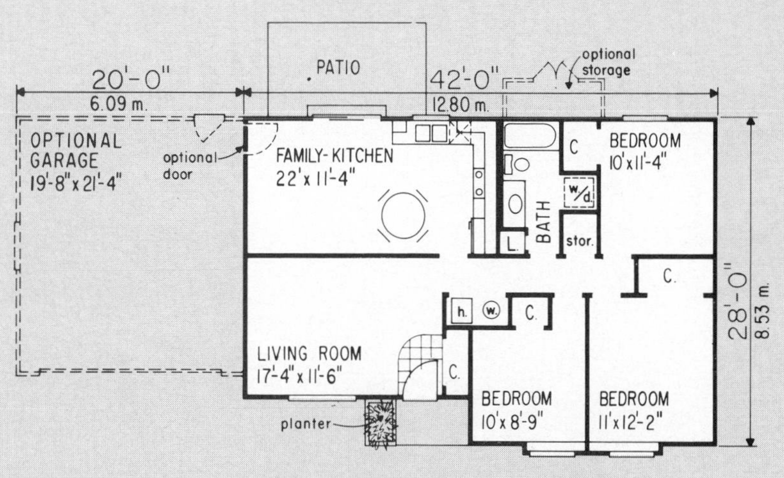

PLAN 2 WITHOUT BASEMENT

Artists' renderings & floor plans may vary slightly from actual working drawings.

design JONESBORO

ENERGY EFFICIENT HOME
49-1189

Living Area .... 1,120 Sq. Ft.

3 BEDROOM PLAN

PLEASE SPECIFY PLAN 1 OR PLAN 2 WHEN ORDERING BLUEPRINT PLANS.

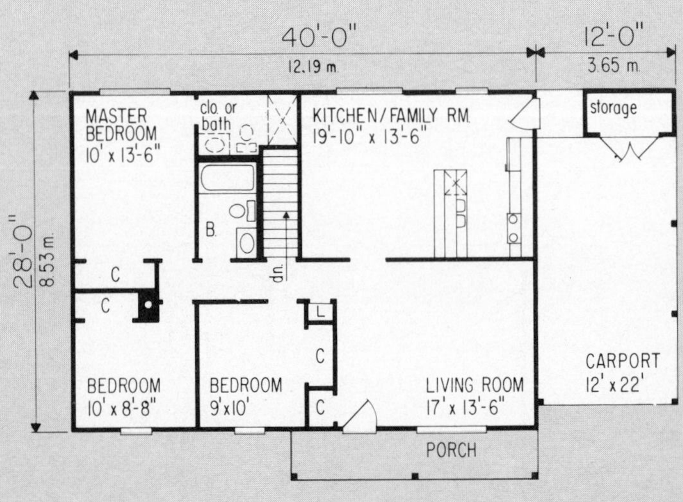

PLAN 1 WITH BASEMENT

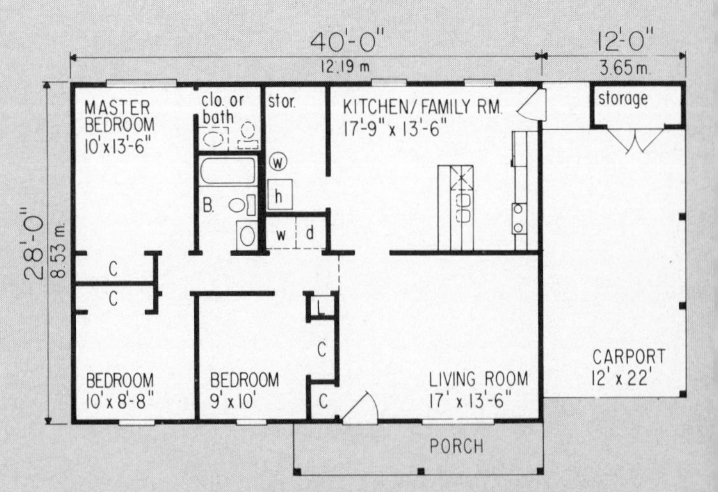

PLAN 2 WITHOUT BASEMENT

Artists' renderings & floor plans may vary slightly from actual working drawings.

Living Area .... 1,120 Sq. Ft.
Future Addition .... 448 Sq. Ft.

PLEASE SPECIFY PLAN 1 OR PLAN 2 WHEN ORDERING BLUEPRINT PLANS.

design PORTLAND

ENERGY EFFICIENT HOME
49-1194

2-3 BEDROOM PLAN

Artists' renderings & floor plans may vary slightly from actual working drawings.

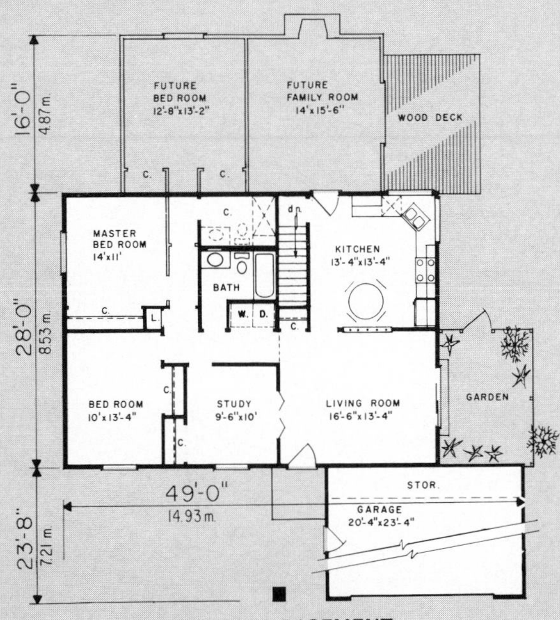

PLAN 1 WITH BASEMENT

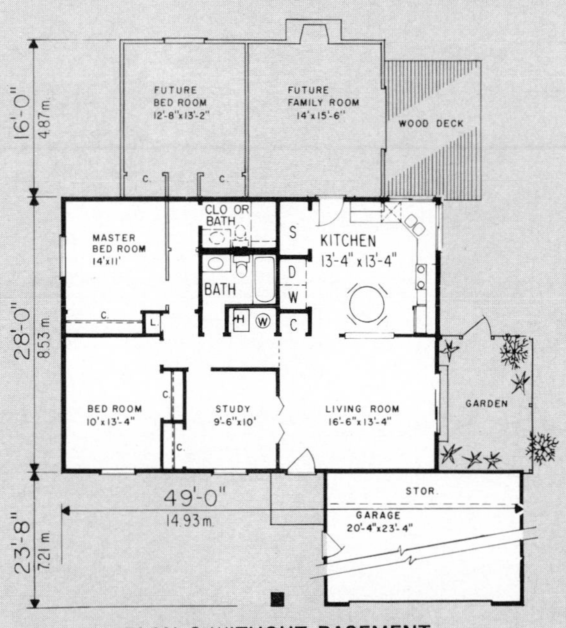

PLAN 2 WITHOUT BASEMENT

design
PRESCOTT
ENERGY EFFICIENT HOME
49-1195

3 BEDROOM PLAN

Living Area
Plan 1 or 2 .... 1,120 Sq. Ft.

PLEASE SPECIFY PLAN 1 OR PLAN 2 WHEN ORDERING BLUEPRINT PLANS.

Adapted from a plan by the U.S. Department of Agriculture Cooperative Farm Building Plan Exchange Harold Zorning, Architect

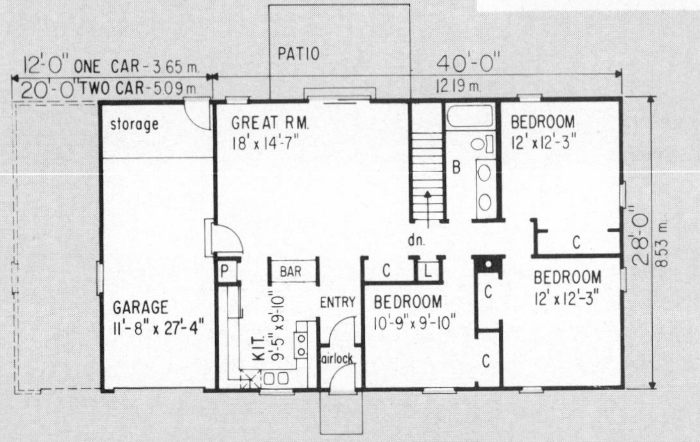

PLAN 1 WITH BASEMENT

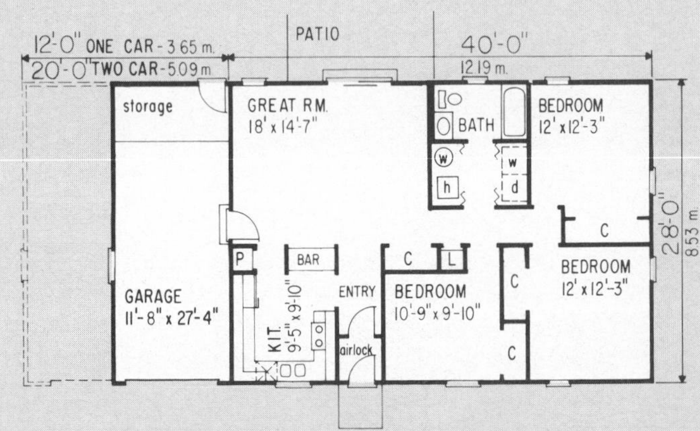

PLAN 2 WITHOUT BASEMENT

design
NEW CASTLE
ENERGY EFFICIENT HOME
49-1196

3 BEDROOM PLAN

Living Area
Plan 1 or 2 .... 960 Sq. Ft.

PLEASE SPECIFY PLAN 1 OR PLAN 2 WHEN ORDERING BLUEPRINT PLANS.

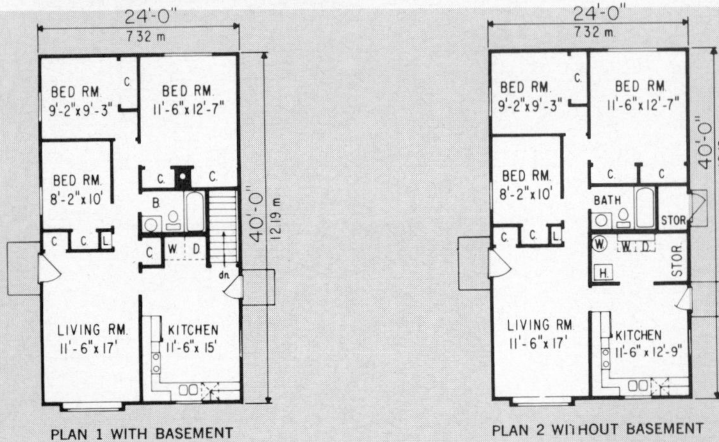

design SHERBROOKE

ENERGY EFFICIENT HOME
49-1197

3 BEDROOM PLAN

Living Area
First Floor .... 768 Sq. Ft.
Second Floor ..... 768 Sq. Ft.

PLEASE SPECIFY PLAN 1 OR PLAN 2 WHEN ORDERING BLUEPRINT PLANS.

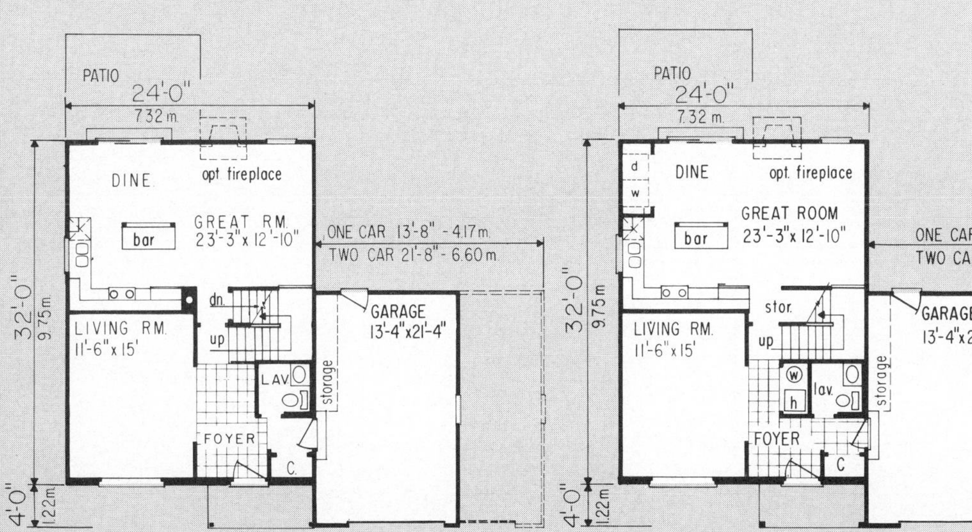

FIRST FLOOR PLAN 1 WITH BASEMENT

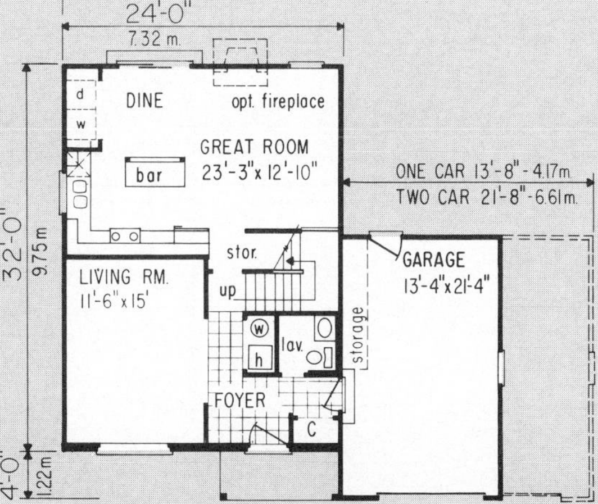

FIRST FLOOR PLAN 2 WITHOUT BASEMENT

BED RM.
11'-6" x 11'
BED RM.
11'-3" x 10'
C.
L
C.
C.
C.
dn.
BATH
flue-
plan 2
MASTER BEDRM.
11'-6" x 15'
BATH

SECOND FLOOR

DESIGN A FRAME CONSTRUCTION WITH BRICK VENEER FRONT

PLEASE SPECIFY DESIGN A OR B AND PLAN 1 OR 2 WHEN ORDERING BLUEPRINT PLANS

design RICHMOND

ENERGY EFFICIENT HOME
49-1198

DUPLEX

2 UNITS - ONE STORY

Living Area: Per Unit
Plan 1 or 2
Design A - ......898 Sq. Ft.
Design B - ......884 Sq. Ft.

DESIGN B ALL FRAME CONSTRUCTION

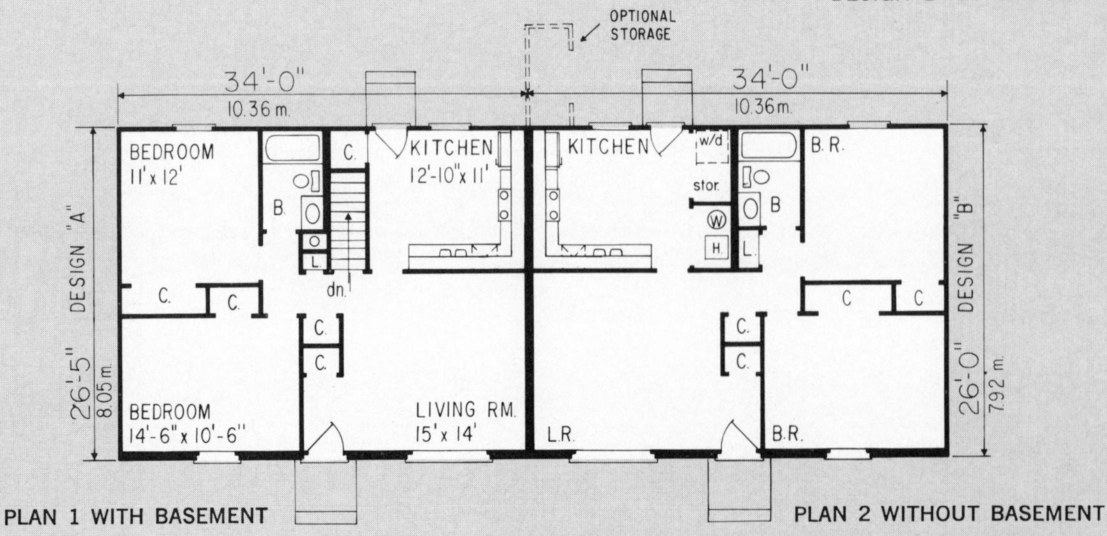

PLAN 1 WITH BASEMENT

PLAN 2 WITHOUT BASEMENT

DUPLEX

design 49-1184

ENERGY EFFICIENT HOME

Living Area per Unit Plan 1 or 2
First Floor .... 554 Sq. Ft.
Second Floor .... 469 Sq. Ft.

- Duplex unit or can be grouped together as townhouses.
- Small in size but big on livability.
- Sheltered entrance.
- Spacious living room and country-sized kitchen.

FOUR UNIT TOWNHOUSE

PLEASE SPECIFY PLAN 1 OR PLAN 2 WHEN ORDERING BLUEPRINT PLANS.

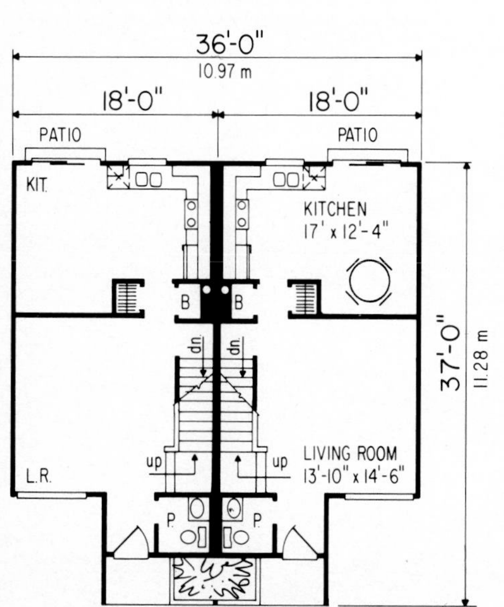

FIRST FLOOR PLAN 1 WITH BASEMENT

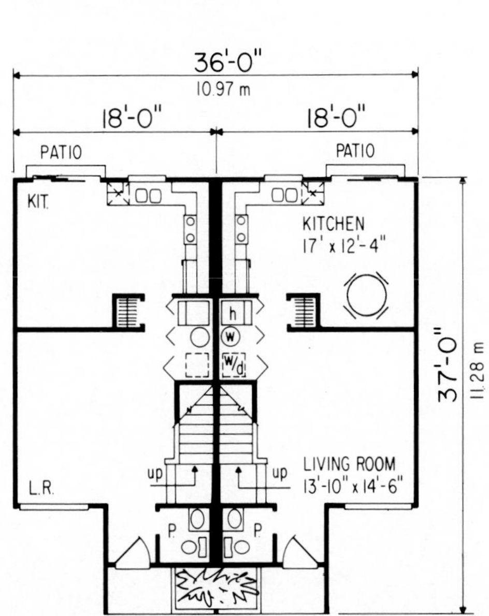

FIRST FLOOR PLAN 2 WITHOUT BASEMENT

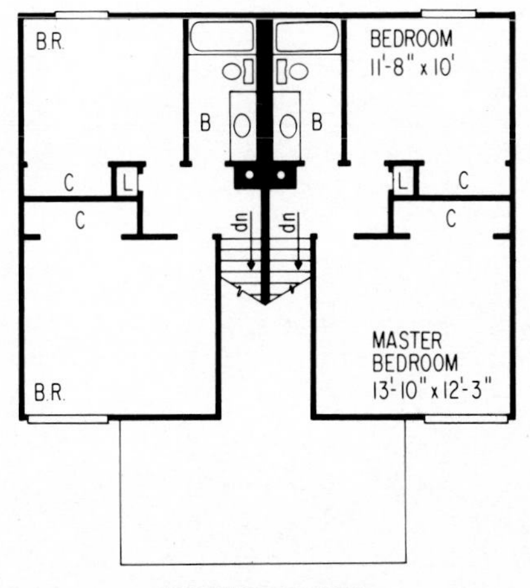

SECOND FLOOR

design

49-1185

ENERGY EFFICIENT HOME

4 BEDROOM PLAN

Living Area
First Floor . . . . 988 Sq. Ft.
Second Floor. . . . . . 520 Sq. Ft.

Artists' renderings & floor plans may vary slightly from actual working drawings.

- A compact contemporary design.
- Room for expansion – finish the first floor now, finish the second floor when needed.
- Deluxe baths on both floors.
- Open living area plan with vaulted living room ceiling.
- Ideal for narrow lot.

BEDROOM 13'-4"x12'-6"
skylight
B.
BEDROOM 12'-6"x12'-6"
dn
C.
C.
open to living room

SECOND FLOOR

N

For maximum Energy Efficiency, we recommend large glass areas to be oriented to the south.

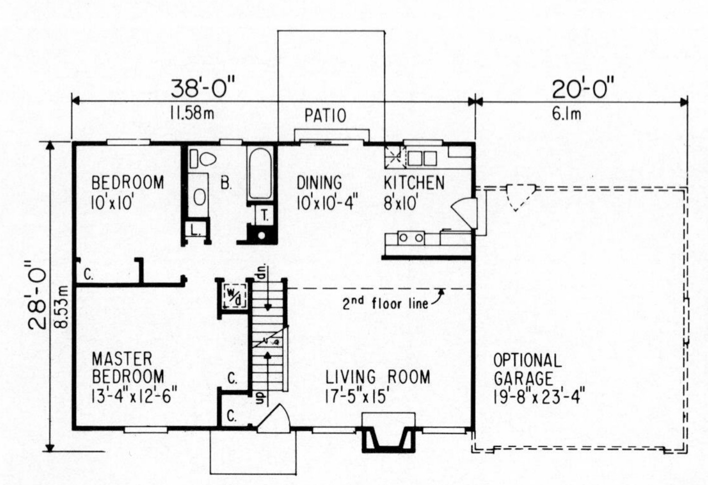

FIRST FLOOR PLAN 1 WITH BASEMENT

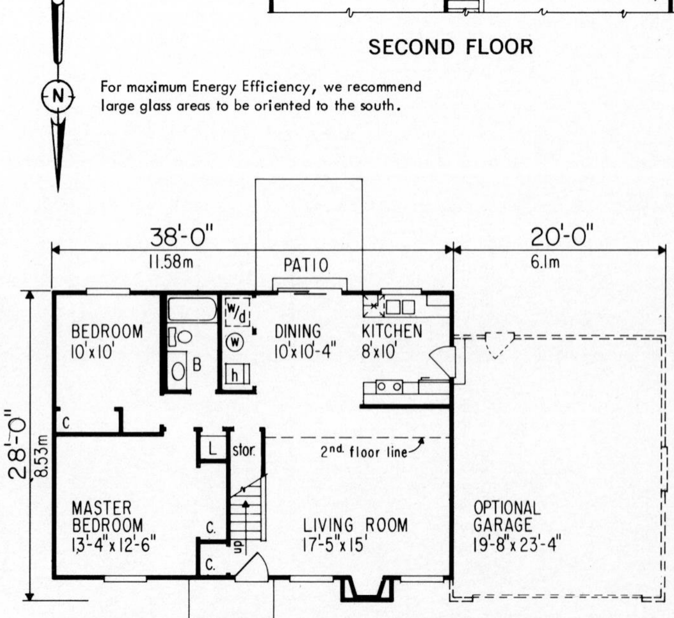

FIRST FLOOR PLAN 2 WITHOUT BASEMENT

design
49-1190

ENERGY EFFICIENT HOME

4 BEDROOM PLAN

Living Area
Plan 1 & 2 . . . . 1,176 Sq. Ft.

PLEASE SPECIFY PLAN 1 OR PLAN 2 WHEN ORDERING BLUEPRINT PLANS.

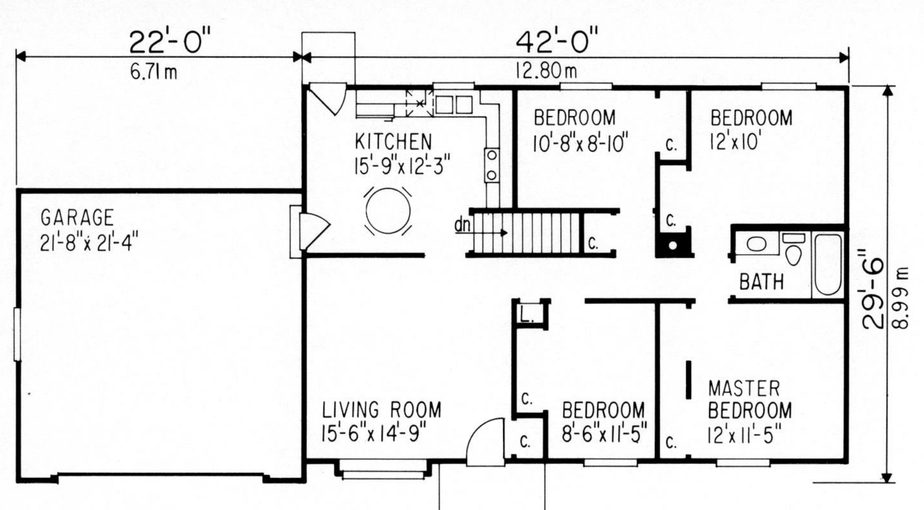

PLAN 1 WITH BASEMENT

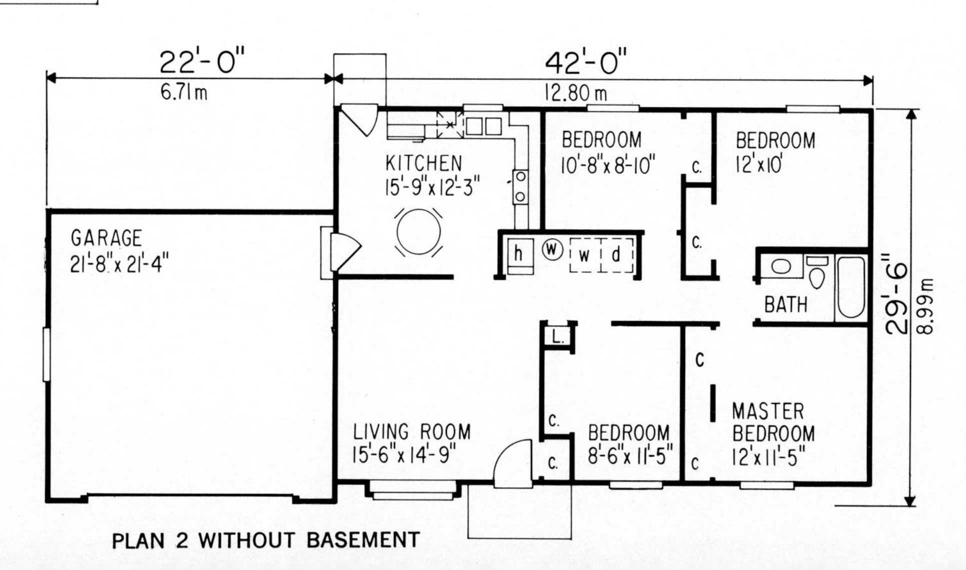

PLAN 2 WITHOUT BASEMENT

Artists' renderings & floor plans may vary slightly from actual working drawings.

design 49-1191

ENERGY EFFICIENT HOME

Living Area
Plan 1 & 2 . . . . 1,186 Sq. Ft.

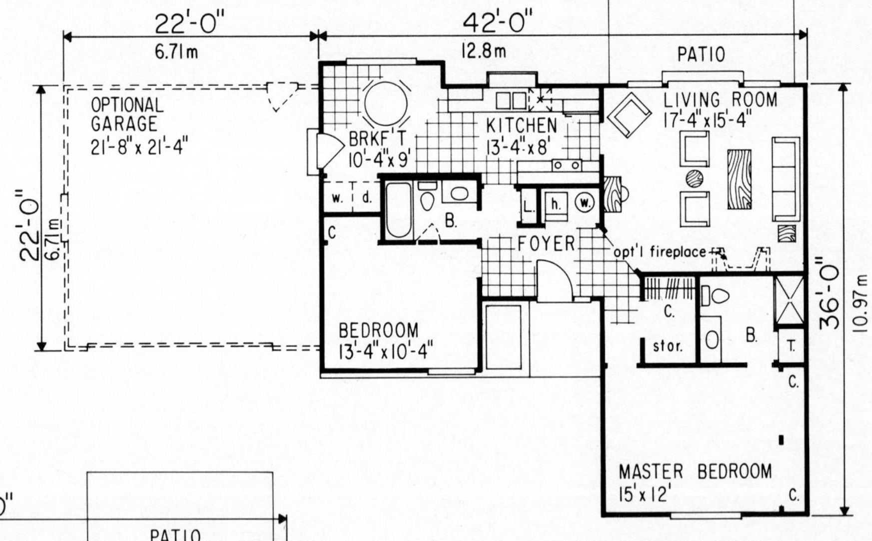

PLAN 2 WITHOUT BASEMENT

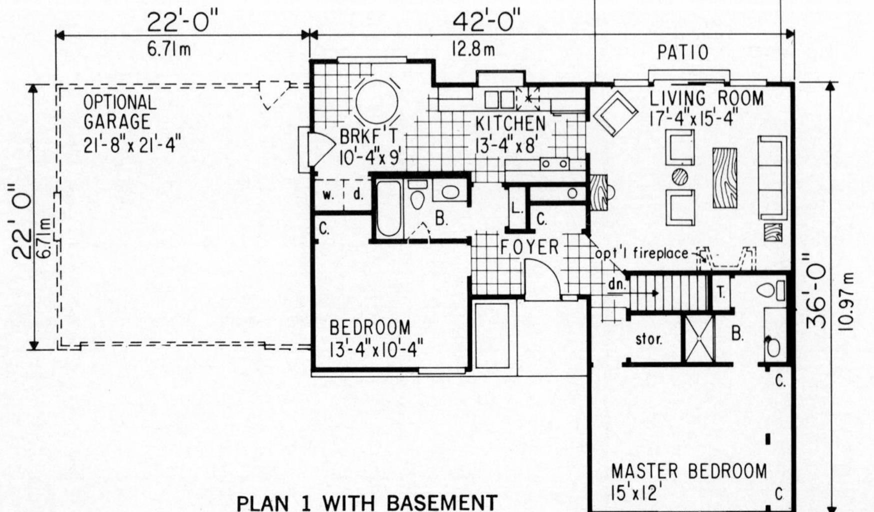

PLAN 1 WITH BASEMENT

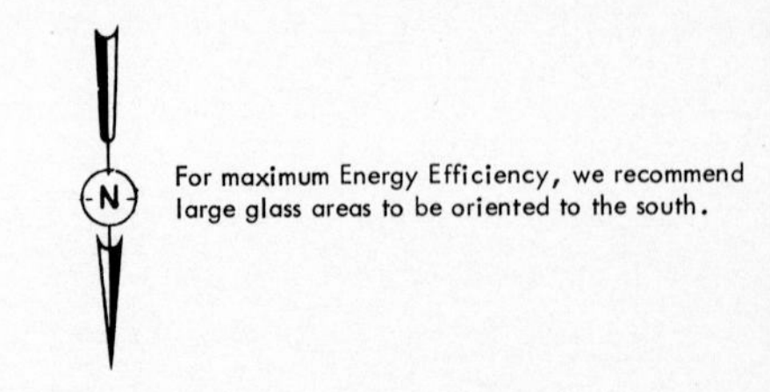

For maximum Energy Efficiency, we recommend large glass areas to be oriented to the south.

PLEASE SPECIFY WITH OR WITHOUT BASEMENT WHEN ORDERING BLUEPRINT PLANS

design 49-1192

ENERGY EFFICIENT HOME

2-3 BEDROOM PLAN

Living Area

Plan 1 & 2 . . . 1,304 Sq. Ft.

PLEASE SPECIFY PLAN 1 OR PLAN 2 WHEN ORDERING BLUEPRINT PLANS.

For maximum Energy Efficiency, we recommend large glass areas to be oriented to the south.

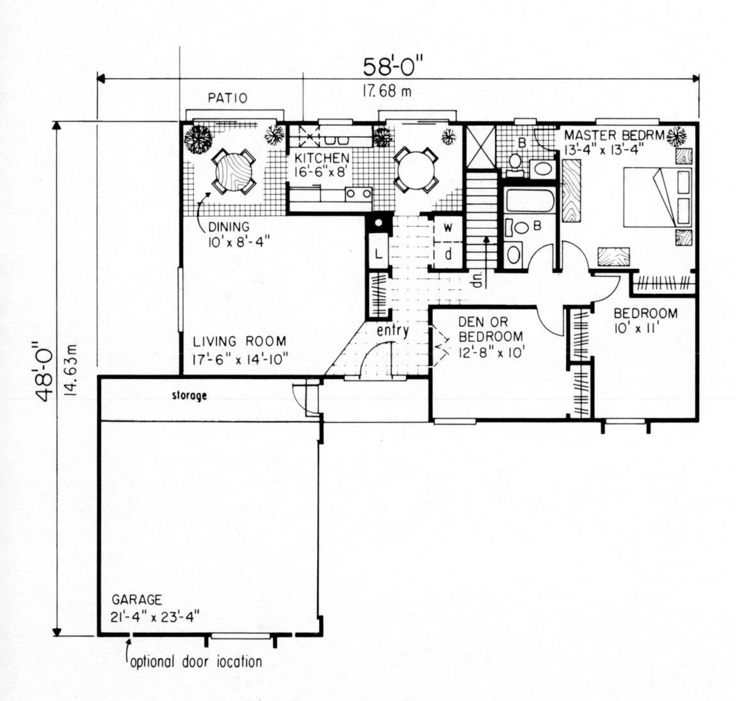

PLAN 1 WITH BASEMENT

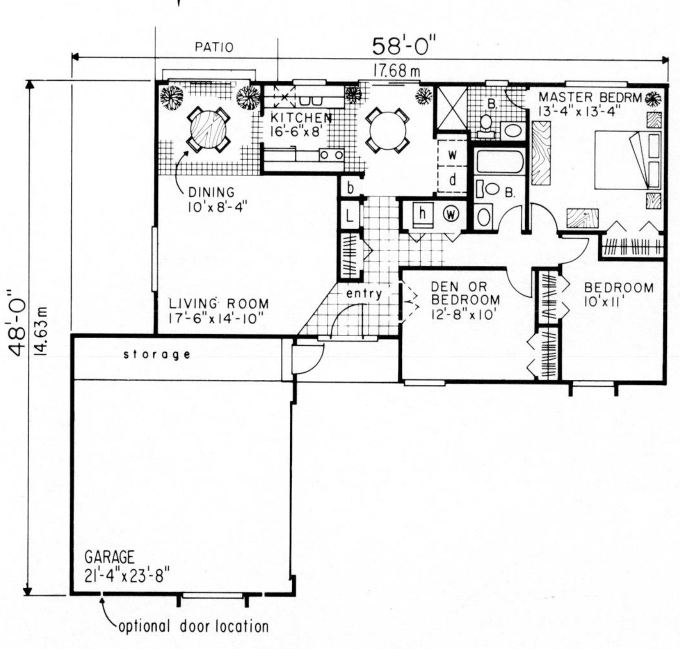

PLAN 2 WITHOUT BASEMENT

design

49-1193

ENERGY EFFICIENT HOME

3 BEDROOM PLAN

Living Area
Plan 1 & 2 . . . . 1,176 Sq. Ft

PLEASE SPECIFY PLAN 1 OR PLAN 2 WHEN ORDERING BLUEPRINT PLANS.

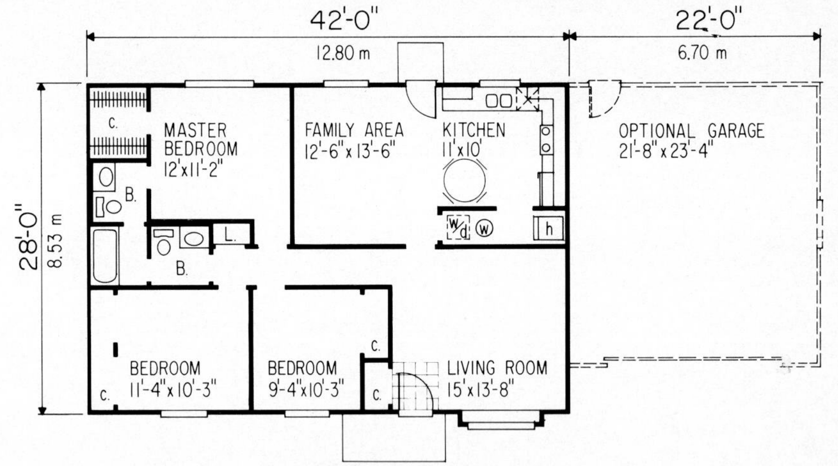

PLAN 2 WITHOUT BASEMENT

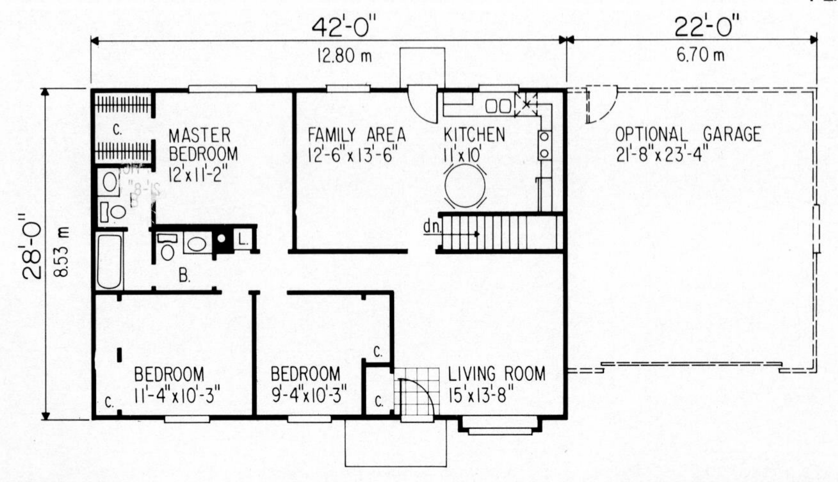

PLAN 1 WITH BASEMENT

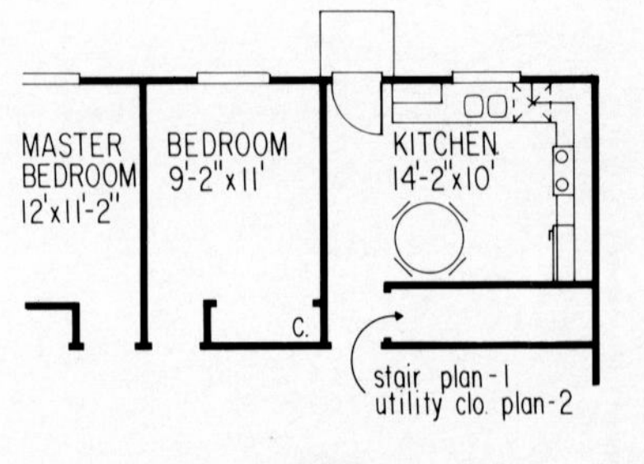

ALTERNATE 4th [illegible]ROOM PLAN

Artists' renderings & floor plans may vary slightly from actual working drawings.

PLEASE SPECIFY PLAN 1 OR PLAN 2 WHEN ORDERING BLUEPRINT PLANS.

design
49-1199

ENERGY EFFICIENT HOME

3 BEDROOM PLAN

Living Area
Plan 1 & 2 . . . . 1,200 Sq. Ft.

Artists' renderings & floor plans may vary slightly from actual working drawings.

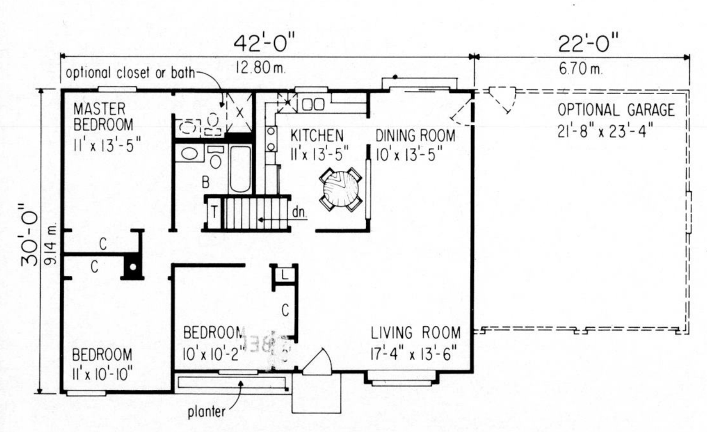

PLAN 1 WITH BASEMENT

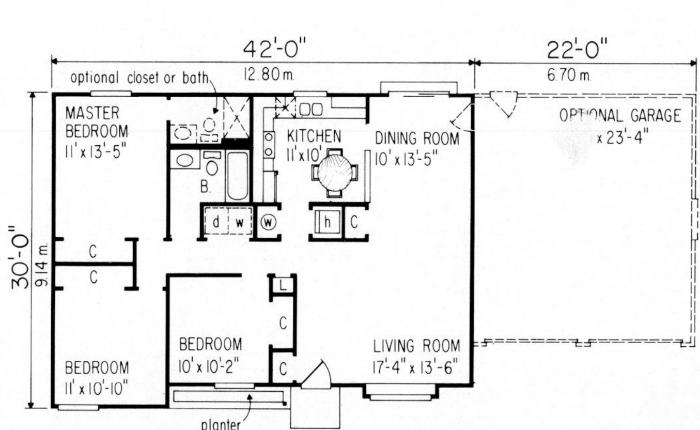

PLAN 2 WITHOUT BASEMENT

A Passive Solar Home . . . The "SOLAR RIDGEWAY"

Sponsored by
The Mid-American Solar Energy Complex (MASEC)

Helping to keep heating costs down in Solar Ridgeway are south-facing windows, thermal storage walls, quarry tile floor areas, earth berms, buffer zones. Glass area is protected from summer sun by an overhang.

If your heating bills are out of this world, and you're planning to build a new home, you really should consider a house like the one shown here.

Photos: Hedrich-Blessing

The secret behind the easy warmup: The sun supplies about half the heating needs; a small, auxiliary, gas-fired furnace the rest.

The home has a carefully designed passive solar-heating system with features you should consider if you plan to build a new home in these days of rising fuel costs.

About passive solar energy

A passive solar-energy system has no moving parts, nothing to wear out or maintain. The Solar Ridgeway is a good example of the Direct Gain type of passive solar heating. This means, simply, that large south-facing windows permit the sun's rays to penetrate deeply into the home and strike thermal storage masses. Here heat is stored for two reasons: First the thermal mass, which in the Solar Ridgeway consists of two massive concrete filled masonry block walls, absorbs and stores solar heat during the day, and thus controls and limits overheating. Second, the stored solar heat is released slowly from the thermal storage mass walls to warm the home at night and on cloudy days.

Solar-Ridgeway is a three-bedroom, split-level house. Note that non-living spaces are located on the north side of the house to act as a buffer from cold northerly wind.

Living room, shown above, has a 12-foot ceiling. Tile floor near windows stores heat for release at night and on cloudy days. Design by Architectural Alliance.

"SOLAR RIDGEWAY"

ENERGY EFFICIENT HOME
49-27001

Living Area
Main & Upper Level—1,394 Sq. Ft.
Lower Level—698 Sq. Ft.

This home's orientation may vary up to 30° east or west of true north without greatly affecting the expected solar contribution.

WOOD

TILE

CONCRETE BLOCK

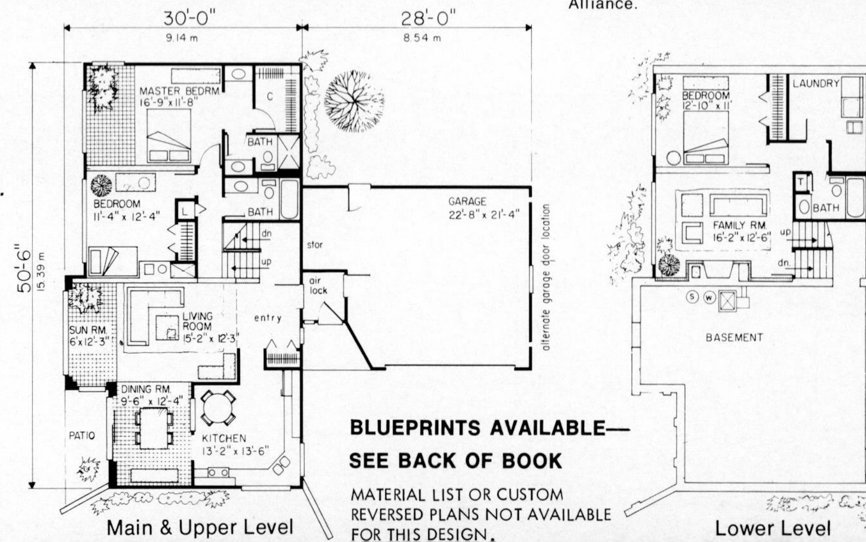

Main & Upper Level

Lower Level

BLUEPRINTS AVAILABLE— SEE BACK OF BOOK

MATERIAL LIST OR CUSTOM REVERSED PLANS NOT AVAILABLE FOR THIS DESIGN.